Famous *Children*

LEONARDO DA VINCI

TONY HART & SUSAN HELLARD

On the day that Leonardo da Vinci was born his proud grandfather, Antonio, wrote in his family records, "Saturday, April 15th at 10.30 pm, 1452, there was born to me a grandson, the child of Ser Piero, my son." Leonardo was born in a tiny village near a town called Vinci in Italy. His family had taken the name of the town as their surname.

Leonardo's parents did not marry each other and so, although he spent his first months being nursed by his mother, Leonardo soon went to live with his father's parents, Antonio and Monna Lucia da Vinci.

"It is such a pleasure to have a young baby in the house again," sighed Monna Lucia happily.

Leonardo's father, Ser Piero, was a busy lawyer. He soon married and was often away from the village, working in Florence. His mother lived nearby and even when she was married, Leonardo would often visit her and her growing family.

Leonardo's uncle, Francesco, looked after the family estate and when he was still very young Leonardo went everywhere with him, tending the olive trees and grape vines and learning a love of nature.

When Leonardo was only four years old he watched with his uncle as a hurricane tore through the countryside, destroying everything in its path. Leonardo never forgot the experience and throughout his life he was fascinated by weather and the power of nature.

Leonardo, an attractive child, was born with remarkable gifts. His mind was always busy and he would set himself many things to learn, never pausing from one subject to the next.

Leonardo carried notebooks with him everywhere he went and was forever scribbling. He had a strange way of writing with his left hand – from right to left and back to front. The only way to read it easily was with a mirror!

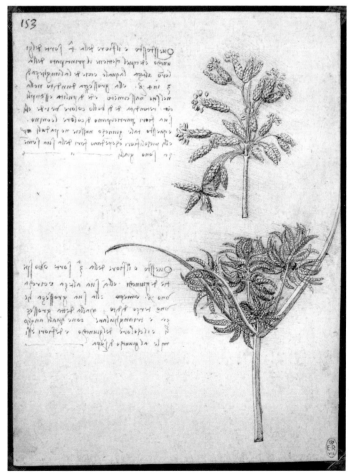

Leonardo had only a limited education in Vinci but his great talents were obvious to his teachers.

"I cannot teach you any more about mathematics, Leonardo," said his baffled teacher, "I have taught you all I know."

He took music lessons and learned to play the lyre. Soon he was writing his own songs.

"I have never heard such good verse and lovely singing," said his music teacher.

Leonardo not only wrote in his notebooks. From an early age he did wonderful drawings to record his thoughts and observations as he roamed the beautiful Italian countryside.

Eventually even his father, Ser Piero, realized that Leonardo's drawings were special. He took some of them

to show to his close friend, Andrea del Verrocchio, who ran a successful artists' workshop in Florence.

"Do you think it's worth allowing Leonardo to study design?" asked Ser Piero.

Verrocchio was amazed by the drawings and urged Piero to bring his son to the workshop. Leonardo was delighted to hear the news.

"Florence will seem very big and strange after living in a village," Leonardo said, "but I can't wait to see it and to learn so many new things."

So, at twelve years old, Leonardo joined his father in Florence, in a house overlooking the government offices where Ser Piero worked.

At Verrocchio's workshop Leonardo began by running errands and sweeping up. But soon he was stretching canvases and making brushes and paints.

Everyone at the workshop learned to draw from life. Leonardo soon attracted his master's attention. He made clay models and draped the figures with cloth dipped in plaster which hardened.

"Now I have folds that will last. I can draw them as they really are," he explained.

"What a good idea," said Verrocchio. "We must learn to draw what we see."

If Leonardo saw a face he wanted to draw he would follow the person all day long until he could remember them exactly. Then he would rush home to make his drawing, just as though the person was still there.

"An artist must be like a mirror," he would say, "reflecting what is placed right in front of it."

Leonardo loved being at the workshop and found Florence an exciting place to live.

In the winter of 1466 a flood surged through the city in the middle of the night. Houses and churches were engulfed. Horses were drowned in their stables. It was soon over but the devastation was dreadful to see. Once again Leonardo was reminded of the power of nature's forces.

At about this time, Florence suffered another bout of the plague. Lorenzo de Medici, its ruler, decided it was time to cheer up everyone and arranged lots of parties and festivities. Verrocchio's studio had to help with the many banners and costumes.

"Can you design a helmet for the Duke of Milan?" Verrocchio asked Leonardo. Leonardo produced a wonderful design.

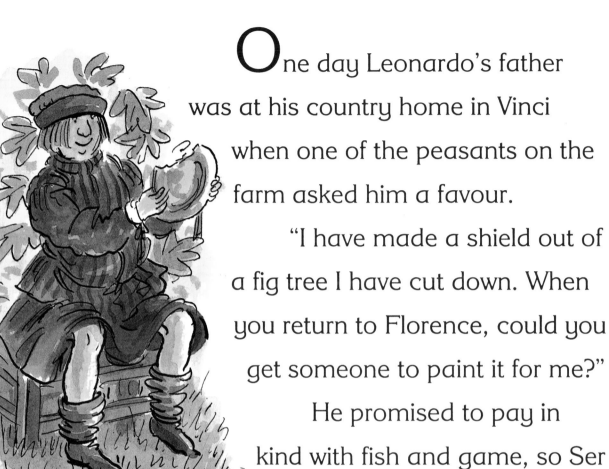

One day Leonardo's father was at his country home in Vinci when one of the peasants on the farm asked him a favour.

"I have made a shield out of a fig tree I have cut down. When you return to Florence, could you get someone to paint it for me?"

He promised to pay in kind with fish and game, so Ser Piero agreed.

When Leonardo saw the shield he said,

"I cannot paint on that, I shall have to re-shape and polish it first."

He transformed the shield into a beautiful object. Then he thought carefully about the design he would paint on it.

"I know, I shall invent my own creature," said Leonardo. "I shall make studies of live lizards, snakes and bats and put them together to make a terrifying monster."

When Ser Piero saw the shield he jumped with horror. He thought it was a real monster.

"Good!" said Leonardo. "The shield has done what it should, and frightened you. Now you can take it."

Verrocchio asked for Leonardo's help with a large painting for the monastery at San Salvi.

Leonardo was allowed to paint the angel carrying Christ's garment. For such a young man, Leonardo's painting was excellent.

"Your painting is beautiful, Leonardo. It is even better than mine. I shall never use paints again," vowed Verrocchio.

To the delight of Leonardo and Ser Piero he made Leonardo his partner.

Leonardo loved animals and when he was twenty he became a vegetarian. He would buy caged birds just so that he could set them free. He loved to study and draw birds in flight.

"I wish I could fly," he thought, so he designed a flying machine with flapping wings and one like a helicopter.

Leonardo was a great inventor – he drew plans for a bicycle 300 years before the first one was built.

He even wrote to the Duke of Milan, "Most illustrious Lord, I have invented thirty-six ways of helping you with your military engineering..."

One of his ideas was a tank!